The Ring

EILEEN DISTASIO-CLARK

Copyright © 2024
All Rights Reserved

With Great Love and Appreciation to Those Who Have and Do Bless My Life.

My Family:

Joseph DeStasio Sr. & Miriam Lucille Baragone DeStasio, My Late Parents.

Andrea Jean DeStasio McIntosh, My Older Sister and Their Families.

Joseph DeStasio Jr., My Younger and Only Brother and Their Families.

Donna Marie DeStasio Wagner, My Younger Sister and Their Families.

My Children:

Eileen, Rebekah, Rachel, S. Michael,

Jennifer, Sharon, Tara, Stephanie,

Apryll, Mikaelah, & M. Trevor

and THEIR Families!!

ACKNOWLEDGEMENTS

First and foremost, I express, deeply, my sincere gratitude to our Heavenly Father for blessing me with the gift and talent of writing! I know I could not do what I do without His assistance.

I also want to acknowledge and express gratitude to the members of my birth family—Joseph Sr., Miriam, Andrea, Joseph Junior, and Donna. All the experiences of my childhood years, experiences that taught me so very much and enabled me to reveal my true self to myself, came about through my experiences and relationships with them.

And, of course, it goes without saying, but I will say it anyway: I also want to acknowledge and note my gratitude to my children, Eileen, Rebekah, Rachel, S. Michael, Jennifer, Sharon, Tara, Stephanie, Apryll, Mikaelah, and M. Trevor, and their families! Through multiple things they said to me, over multiple years, I finally came to the realization that

Heavenly Father gave me the gift of writing and opened the doors to these experiences because He knew that by sharing them with others, others could feel His love too.

And He definitely wants us all to know that He, Heavenly Father, Heavenly Mother, and Jehovah truly do loves us!!!

INTRODUCTION

There are sixteen books in this series, which I refer to as *"The Ellie Series."* All of the characters in these stories portray real people from my life. The main characters depict the members of my family: Daddy is my daddy; Mommy is my mommy; Jeannic is my older sister; Junior is my brother; Maria is my younger sister, and Ellie is me. Now, those are not our actual first names, but they do reference us.

The first story in the series presents our Heavenly Father's Plan of Salvation and takes place in the Pre-Earth World. Now, of course, because we all—when we were born—received what is known as The Veil of Forgetfulness, I do not actually remember everything from or about the Pre-Earth World, but I do know about and understand it from much study and worship as a member of The Church of Jesus Christ of Latter-Day Saints, and memories restored to me through the Holy Spirit. So, from this story there is much truth to be learned.

The last story in the series is set in the Post-Mortal World, and presents a depiction of what happens to us after this life. Again, because I have not gone there yet, I cannot say I 'remember' this. But, I have also learned about the Post-Mortal World from much study and worship as a member of The Church of Jesus Christ of Latter-Day Saints.

All of the other stories are based on true events from my life; events that actually occurred when and how they are depicted in these stories. I chose these events because they are among the many occurrences in my life that presented—or revealed that which I already knew without having to be taught—Principles of Eternal Truths.

Also, I chose these events as the settings for my stories because they depict wonderful learning moments from my childhood and adolescent years, lessons that have blessed and benefited me throughout the whole of my life and will forever continue to do so. Also, through these great truths and their consequences in my life, I have been able to share them with many others, whose lives have also been blessed by them.

So, please, read and enjoy, then care and share the messages and stories with others!!

Now, there are also a couple of things you can look for:

In each story, the title of the previous story is presented in *italicized* form, the title of the next story is presented in *Capitalized Italicized* form, and the title of the story being read is presented in **emboldened** form.

Also, every story has at least one word that is uncommon or 'created.'

So, as you read, search, find, and have fun!

THE RING

If there was ever anything that Ellie loved more than anything else, it was horses and everything related to them: saddles—especially the ones made out of black leather—bridles and bits, and horseshoes—the shinier, the better—cowboy boots and hats, as long as she did not have to wear them, ropes and lassoes, sheriffs' stars and deputies' badges, stables, stalls, and... well, you get the idea, everything!

Mommy always told Ellie, "For a little sweetheart, you sure are picky!"

Yep, Ellie loved them all! And yep, there was just about nothing, if there was anything at all, well, except for God and her family that Ellie loved more than horses!

There was nothing she wanted more than to have a horse. Ask her what she wanted for her birthday, and she would say a horse! Ask her what she desired for Christmas, and she would say a horse. Ask her what she needed for any time or any reason, and she would say a horse.

So, of course, it was to be expected that she would be spilling over with excitement when she found that beautiful horseshoe ring! It was a really shiny yellow-gold ring, shaped like a horseshoe, with super shiny diamonds, and it just about almost came close to fitting her fattest finger, which was the thumb on her right hand. So excited was she that she found herself standing beside herself with happiness. It was the greatest thing that ever happened to her, until the next greatest thing that ever happened to her happened, and this is how it happened.

It was late in aut...

Uhhhh, hold on one minute! Let me explain something else about Ellie that should help to make this explanation make more sense. Ellie liked to find things. Whenever she took a walk anywhere, to school, to church, to her relatives' houses, to the playground or the pool, to the store or to... well, let me keep this short and just say, to anywhere, she would look at the ground, the trees, the bushes, whatever was around her, in hopes of finding 'a treasure.'

Now, exactly what Ellie thought a treasure was, I do not know. I do not know if she knew. But what I do know is that she always looked and looked, and loo... okay, so you get the idea, she always looked for something to find. And every time she found something, she bubbled over with excitement, ran home—when it was time to go home from wherever she had gone—and gleefully displayed it for all her family to see.

One of her favorite finds was a coin that she had found on the street, Chestnut Street, the street where she lived, just half a block up from her house, when she was crossing the street to go to the corner store to pick up some things that her mommy had ordered. Being only six years old, she could not identify what kind of a coin it was; she just knew it was not a penny because it was not the color of a penny. But it was a coin, and it was on the ground, and there was no one around to claim it. So, she picked it up, wiped it clean, well, as clean as she could get it using the edge of her shirt, looked at both sides, then stuffed it into her pocket and took it home. Of course, she showed it to everyone, but especially to Daddy, who collected coins.

In fact, collecting and sorting coins was something that Ellie always enjoyed doing with Daddy. So, that made this find all the more special. In fact, in Ellie's mind, it was the best thing that she had ever found. In double fact, to Ellie, it was the best thing that anyone could ever have found! At least, that was what she thought until…

It was late in the early evening, on a cool and gloomy October Tuesday. The clouds were hanging around, like they almost always, always did, cluttering the sky and hiding the sun, the one Ellie said she had learned about in school, but only sometimes saw. It seemed to her that the Pennsylvania sky was pretty shy; it often hid behind the clouds. She should have been used to the gloom; after all, she had never lived anywhere else, but still, she was not; she preferred the sun. But right then, she did not care about the sun or the clouds, she just wanted to go home, sit under *the tree in their backyard,* until dinner was ready, and tell the angels that sat on the highest branches all about her day.

Bursting through the church doors, reverently of course, she bounded down the Franklin Street stairs and darted around the kids in front of her, making her way to the corner. Now, normally, since Sister Elizabeth, Ellie's second-year Catechism teacher, always let her class leave on time, Ellie just waited for Jeannie by the door, because Sister Rose, Jeannie's fourth-grade Catechism, never let her class out on time. But that day, since everyone was getting out a little later than usual, for no particular reason that Ellie could see, she was in an even bigger hurry to get home. Now, again, you may be wondering why. Well, this is why...

It was Tuesday, and it was autumn, and that meant the Stations—Ellie's family—were having homemade macaroni soup, and that meant Ellie would be eating without a fuss, and that meant she would not have to go to bed early. She liked macaroni soup; well... at least she disliked it a lot less than she disliked almost everything else, so she was in a hurry to get home.

But then, I guess she would have been in a hurry to get home even if they were not having macaroni soup, and not for any particular reason. Ellie was always in a hurry to get home. She loved being at home with her family. Of course, even if she were not headed home, she probably would still have been in a hurry because she was always in a hurry to get everywhere.

Just as she was about to step down off the curb to cross 7th Avenue, she heard Jeannie calling from behind, "Ellie, wait for me!"

"Hurry up!" Ellie called over her shoulder, almost stopping, but really, just slowing down. She was jumping up onto the far curb when Jeannie caught up with her.

"You know you are supposed to wait for me," she reminded Ellie.

"Yeah, yeah, I know," Ellie replied, unaffected by Jeannie's reminder.

"Can't you walk like a normal person," Jeannie asked when Ellie bumped into her while jumping over a line.

"No!" Ellie replied emphatically, "I want to live forever! I cannot take any chances."

"What are you talking about?" Jeannie asked in a tone that seemed to suggest that Ellie was from some distant planet and did not speak English.

"You know," Ellie said, hardly able to believe that Jeannie was asking such a question. Then in her best 'teacher voice,' she recited the silly, bumfuzzling, chucklesome rhyme that their older cousins had taught them; "Step on a crack, break your mother's back; step on a line, die at thirty-nine."

Well, after that, even though she was quite amused, Jeanie tried to make it look like she was annoyed, by walking faster. Now, that was okay with Ellie, because that gave her a reason to run, which she did, for about twenty feet; then she found out, again, why running was not usually a good idea for a less than graceful, sometimes clumsy, seven-year-old pint-sized squirt.

Uh, Side Note: That was what everyone called her, a pint-sized squirt, because she was much smaller than just about everyone else. But from Ellie's view, she was not a pint-sized squirt. It was everyone else who was a water-tower-sized giant. Now, back to the other side.

Anyway, with all the poise and grace of a football player in a tackle, Ellie tripped over herself, tumbled to the ground like Jack and Jill with their pail of water, and rolled a quarter turn into a pile of leaves the size of Rhode Island.

"Oh, man," she moaned, gazing up at the gray clouds, through the naked branches of Mr. Meany's sycamore tree. Mr. Meany was not really his name; Ellie did not know his real name, but Mr. Meany was what all the kids called him because he was always yelling at them, for anything, everything, and nothing at all. And there she was, lying on his lawn, in his pile of newly raked leaves.

Now, you may be wondering, 'How did she know they were his leaves?' Well, I will tell you how she knew. She had seen him raking them when she was on her way to Catechism. That was how she knew they were his. Oh, and of course, she knew they were his because she knew he was the one who lived in that house. And, knowing that it was his lawn, she was certain that death by Meany's screaming would be her fate if he caught her lying in his leaves.

***Uh! Another Side Note Here: You may have noticed by now; Ellie has a tendency to be a little dramatic about things, especially little things. With big things, things that really were more serious, she had a different tendency. With those things, she was more likely to downsize them. But the little things?

Well, to her, it seemed she thought they were world-ending! Now, back to the other side.***

"Why does this always happen to me?" Ellie groaned to herself.

"Are you okay?" Jeannie asked with concern, as she came running back. "What happened?"

"I think I fell," Ellie said playfully, as she helped herself up. "I tripped over me."

"Are you okay?" Jeannie asked again, with what sounded like genuine concern.

"Yeah, I am fine," Ellie assured her, as she brushed the crumpled red and brown leaves and the yellow grass off of her coat. It was when she bent down to brush the leaves and grass off of her tights that she saw it. It was laying there, in all its splendor, right where she had been laying, in the bed of leaves.

"Wow," she whispered as she picked up a ring and examined it. "Wow! Wow!" she exclaimed, as she tried it on all ten fingers. "Wow! Wow! Wow!" she shouted, as she handed it to Jeannie, "Look what I found!"

"WOW!" Jeannie echoed, "That's really pretty!"

"Yeah," Ellie agreed, "but better than that, it is a horseshoe!"

"Oh my gosh," Jeannie said in disbelief, as she handed it back to Ellie, "You're crazy."

"You bet," Ellie agreed proudly, "crazy about horses!"

As they walked the last five, of the five and a half blocks between their house and the church, they mused over Ellie's newfound 'treasure.'

"Who do you think lost it?" Ellie asked. "Surely, Mr. Meany would not have a ring like this one. He is not nice enough to like horses."

Jeannie chuckled a little at Ellie's reasoning and said, "No, he probably wouldn't. I think you might be right." Then, after looking at the ring a second time, she said, "You know, Ellie, rings do not usually just fall off of people's fingers, at least not without them knowing it. So, how do you think he lost it?"

"What makes you think it was a boy who lost this ring?" Ellie asked, somewhat offended by the thought.

"A girl wouldn't wear a ring like that!" Jeannie said.

"I would!" Ellie replied with indignation, not that she knew what that meant.

"Oh... well..." Jeannie paused thoughtfully and then asked, "Do you think it is real?

"Sure!" Ellie said, as if Jeannie had asked a silly question.

"Why?" Jeannie wanted to know.

"Because it looks real," Ellie explained matter-of-factly.

"And how would you know what a real gold ring looks like?" Jeannie asked.

"I have seen Mommy's and Daddy's rings," Ellie replied.

"Oh, yeah…" Jeannie said. Then after another short pause, she asked, "Do you think they'll let you keep it?"

"Sure!" Ellie replied, as if Jeannie had asked another silly question, and then she asked, "Why would they not?"

In a somewhat teasing tone that suggested that it was Ellie's question that was a rather silly one, Jeannie said, "Because, you know, Daddy doesn't believe in 'finders… keepers… losers… weepers.'"

"Oh, yeah… well… I guess we will see," was the only thing Ellie could think of to say.

Once they got home, before she did anything else, Ellie showed **the ring** to everyone, to Mommy, who was making dinner. To Junior and Maria, who were watching some cartoons on TV. To Daddy, who was watching Junior and Maria, while he read the newspaper. Of course, they all agreed that it was beautiful, and Ellie was very lucky to have found it.

"Yes," Ellie chimed, "yes, I was very lucky. In fact," she said, as if she was grown up and knew what she was talking about. "This is the greatest thing that has ever happened to me. I would never have gotten a ring like this if I had to buy it."

"You are probably right," Daddy said, after examining it a second time. "This is real gold, and these are real diamonds. A ring like this costs a lot of money—money we don't have—money someone else spent. I wonder…" Daddy handed **the ring** back to Ellie, and then, while continuing to look at her, he leaned back in his favorite, comfy, overstuffed, easy chair and picked up his newspaper.

"Wonder what?" Ellie asked curiously and cautiously.

Daddy did not answer right away, but when he did, he looked deep into Ellie eyes, past her thinking self, into her soul, and spoke to her spirit, to the best part of her. "A ring like this would mean a lot to you, wouldn't it, Ellie?" he asked.

"Yeah," she replied emphatically, knowing that he did not really have to ask her that. She knew that he had to know that it would.

"And if you lost it, you would be very sad, wouldn't you?" he continued.

"Yeah," she replied with even greater emphasis; she knew he had to know that too!

"And if someone else found it, you would want them to return it, wouldn't you?" he asked, but it was not really a question.

"Yeah," Ellie replied less enthusiastically. Now, she was pretty sure she knew where he was going, and she did not want to have to go there too.

"I don't think anybody would spend that much money on a ring that didn't mean a lot to them. Do you?" he asked.

"No," Ellie replied sadly, her head drooping, and her heart slowing down.

"And if they lost it, I would think they would want the person who found it to return it," he continued, "What do you think?"

"I think what you think," Ellie said, very sadly, with her chin very nearly 'touching the floor' and her heart beating in that 'slower than molasses in January,' 'poor me' mode.

"So, I wonder…," Daddy said again, as he leaned a little closer to her.

She knew what he was saying, without saying it; she knew that he thought that she should give **the ring** back to whoever lost it.

"But how would I do that, Daddy?" she asked, as if she had heard his thoughts. "I do not even know who lost it."

"We could put an ad in the paper," he replied, settling back in his chair.

Side Note: Yes, I do mean an ad in the paper kind of newspaper. Remember, Ellie was a little girl, a very little girl, quite some time ago. Now, back to the other side.

"I guess we could," Ellie said softly and sullenly, as she sulked toward the stairs. It was quite obvious that Ellie was sad, sad, sa… well, you get it, all of the excitement she had felt by finding **the ring** was drifting away with the thought that she might not be able to keep **the ring**.

On the first step, she stopped and sighed. On the second step, she paused and cried. On the third step, she stood stone still and thought, and thought, and thou... well, I am sure you know what I mean. She thought for a little bit and then, without turning around or even looking over her shoulder, she asked solemnly, "Do we really have to?"

Daddy sat quietly for a moment then simply said, "Well, Ellie, you know that God wants us to do what is right, and He will always help us to know what that is. So, why don't you ask Him?"

Ellie turned and stared at Daddy for a moment, or two, or three, or . . . well, again, you know where this is going. After staring at him for a bit of time, she replied, "I will," and that night she did, and the greatest thing that ever happened to her, until the next, greatest thing that ever happened to her, happened, and this is how it happened.

Ellie held **the ring** all through dinner; it seemed to make her macaroni soup taste even better than it usually did. Then, she put **the ring** on the bathtub ledge while she took her bath, and was sure that when she was done, she was cleaner than ever. Even her pajamas felt more comfortable.

When it was time to get in bed, she took **the ring**, polished it with her blanket, and carefully put it under her pillow. Then, she knelt down beside her bed to say her prayers. Well, she did not really kneel down beside her bed; she slept on the top bunk. Since she could not kneel in the air, she knelt down beside Jeannie's bed; she slept on the bottom bunk.

After "The Lord's Prayer," "The Apostles' Creed," and ten "Hail Marys", Ellie told Heavenly Father about **the ring**. She told Him how much she would like to keep it. She told Him that Daddy thought she should return it. She also told Him that she did not know who lost it. And, of course, she told Him that she wanted to do what was right, but she did not know what the right choice was. Soooooo, she said…

"If it is okay for me to keep it, then please let it stay under my pillow. When I find it in the morning, I will know that it is mine to keep. But, if it is not okay for me to keep it, then please take it, and give it back to the person who lost it. If it is not under my pillow in the morning, I will know that it was not okay for me to keep it and that You took it and gave it back to the person who lost it. Amen."

Ellie climbed quietly up the ladder and slid silently between the covers. As she laid her head on her pillow, and thought of the beautiful treasure beneath it, she began to imagine what her friends would say when they saw it on her finger, well, on her thumb, the next day. She thought about whom she would show it to first, that would be Dalia, her "bestest" friend, and there was Ryma, and there was Lindy too, they had been good friends to her and she was sure they would be as excited as she was. She did not think she wanted to show it to Willy or Ned; they were always teasing her, but Rey was nice, so he could see it too.

About the time she began to slip into slumber, she thought about how Dalia, Ryma, Lindy, and she would take turns wearing it. Dalia could wear it during Math class, Ryma could wear it when they had Music class, and Lindy could wear it for Reading class. Ellie would ask Miss Retnuh-, their second-grade teacher, to put it in her pocket during recess. She would not want to lose it!

Of course, there would be days when she would let Jeannie wear it too; after all, Jeannie was her sister, and was with her when she found it. In fact, if Jeannie had not been walking so much ahead of her, Ellie might have listened to her and not run. Then she would not have fallen on Mr. Meany's leaves, and she probably would never have seen **the ring**. "Yes," she told herself as she slipped into slumber, "it would be the right thing to do, to share it with Jeannie that is, and I do want to do the right thing."

Ellie awoke to the thump, thump, thump of the broom handle against the dining room ceiling, which was the underside of her bedroom floor, and Mommy's voice calling, "Girls, it's time to get up and get ready for school."

She sat up slowly, stretching and yawning, and rubbing the sleep from her eyes. "It is not time to get up," she moaned, "I must be dreaming." She dropped back down onto her pillow and pulled the covers over her head. She even began to doze off, but...

It was not long before she heard the thumping broom and Mommy's emphatic call..., "Girls, I don't hear your feet on the floor!"

Great galoshes, Ellie thought as she rolled over, *why does morning have to come so early, and why does it have to be so cold in my room?* Wrapping the blankets around herself even tighter, she decided she was not going to get up, at least not yet!

Now, make no mistake, Ellie loved school; she just did not like getting out of her nice warm bed, stepping onto the frozen floor, and, with frost-bitten feet, stumbling into the icebox they called a bathroom to get ready. To Ellie, it was torture, morbid, medieval torture.

So, she slid deeper under the covers where it was warm and cozy, until she heard the third and final thumping of the broom, Mommy never gave them more than three warnings, and Mommy's command, "Girls, I'm not going to tell you again; don't make me come up there!"

Of course, Ellie knew better than to ignore the third and final command, but it was exceptionally cold, and Jeannie had just gone into the bathroom. She knew she had just a little more time, so she pulled her flattened feather pillow over her head, intending to wait for Mommy's footsteps on the stairs, but at that moment, she remembered **the ring**.

She jolted up in one bound, spun around and reached for **the ring**, where her pillow had been. It was not there. She shook her pillow—no ring! She shook it out of its case and turned the case inside out—still no ring!! She searched all over her bed, stripping off all the blankets, one at a time; the sheets, and her clothes, which she kept between the covers so they would be warm when she got dressed, there was no ring anywhere!

She jumped down from the top bunk, forgetting about the time and not even feeling the cold. She began searching Jeannie's bed, tearing off the covers, and emptying her pillow from its case. She thought that perhaps **the ring** had fallen off her bed, onto Jeannie's. After all, when Ellie slept, she stayed about as still as a fish on the end of a hook.

She crawled under the bed and shook each shoe, one at a time, tossing it out onto the middle of the carpet. About the time the last shoe sailed across the room, Jeannie came out of the bathroom. "What are you doing?" she cried.

"Looking for my ring!" Ellie called from under the bed. "I put it under my pillow last night, but it is not there!" She crawled out from under the bed and began pulling and tugging on it to get it away from the wall.

"You're going to be in big trouble," Jeannie warned, then went downstairs for her breakfast.

Ellie did not seem to care about the trouble she might be in, which was quite out of the ordinary for Ellie. She never wanted to be in trouble, but in that moment, what she really wanted, was that ring. Not finding it on the beds, under the bed, or behind the bed, she moved to the dresser at the foot of the bed. She looked on it, in it, behind it, and under it. There was just no ring to be found anywhere.

"What on earth are you doing, young lady?" Daddy gasped, as he entered their room, on his way to the bathroom. "You are supposed to be getting ready for school, not tearing up the place."

"Daddy," Ellie cried. "I cannot find my ring."

As Daddy sat down on the floor beside her, she continued to explain, "I put it under my pillow last night, but now it is gone."

Daddy put his arm around her shoulder and asked tenderly, "Are you sure you did not leave it in a pocket, or your school bag, or maybe someplace else?"

"No, Daddy," Ellie said, between the sniffles, "I know I put it under my pillow, but it is gone!"

Looking around at the thorough mess she had made of the room, he asked gently, "How can you be so sure?"

Ellie told him about how she had put it under her pillow, and then said her prayers before getting in bed. She told him that she had put **the ring** under her pillow because she did not want to forget where it was, and because she needed to have it there for her special prayer.

"Your special prayer?" Daddy asked. "Tell me about that, Ellie. What did you say?"

After a few more sniffles, Ellie began to explain, "I told God that I really wanted to keep **the ring**, but that you said I should give it back. I told Him that I did not know who lost it, and that I really wanted to keep it, but that I also wanted to do what was right. So, I asked Him to take it and give it back... to the person who lost it... if it was not okay for me to keep it, and to leave it under my pillow if it was!"

Even before she finished her explanation, she knew what had happened. Daddy must have known that she knew, maybe by the expression on her face, and she knew there was one because she could feel her face change from 'oh, woe is me' to 'wow, glory be' anyway, he must have known because he smiled, gave her a hug, and then stood up without saying a word.

"He did it, Daddy," Ellie said in awe, "He took **the ring**, and gave it back!"

"Yes," Daddy said simply, "yes, He did, and now," he added while helping her up, "clean up this mess and get ready for school."

"Oh, man," Ellie moaned as she looked around the room, "why do I always do things like this? It will take me three Tuesdays and a June to clean up this mess!"

She placed the shoes back under the bed, the red ones, then the blue ones, then the black… well, you know where this is going, all of them neatly aligned and ordered by size and color, just as they had been. She redressed the bunks—that was a pain—and pushed the bed back against the wall. She picked up all the stuff that she had knocked off the dresser and put it back where it had been, and then she got ready for school.

All that time, she kept thinking about **the ring**, how fantastic it had been to find it, and how much more amazing it had been to lose it. It was so amazing because God had done it!

He had taken **the ring** and returned it to its owner. Ellie knew that she did not know how He did it, but she knew that she knew that He did do it. And she knew why He did it!

It really was the right thing to do, to give it back to the person who lost it, the person who bought it, and after all, that was really what she wanted most, more than anything else. Even more than she wanted the beautiful gold and diamond horseshoe ring, she wanted to do what was right, and that was *Something to Be Proud Of*.

As she headed downstairs for breakfast, she thought aloud, "God did it! He helped me do the right thing. This is the greatest thing that has ever happened to me!" And perhaps up to then, it was, but certainly, it was only the greatest thing that had ever happened to her until the next greatest thing that ever happened to her, happens and who knows how that will happen. Yes, Ellie began that day grateful that she had both found and 'lost' **the ring**.

ABOUT THE AUTHOR

Eileen DiStasio-Clark is the second oldest of four children. She is the mother of eleven children and grandmother to twenty-three grandchildren, to date. As a member of The Church of Jesus Christ of Latter-Day Saints, she serves in various positions, teaching, leading, and ministering to children, youth, and adults. Currently, she is also a Family History Missionary. Eileen established the Pursuit of Excellence Institute of Family Education, a non-profit organization focused on strengthening the family. Presently she holds an AA, a BA, and an MA in Clinical Psychology and is working on the completion of her Doctoral Degree.

www.ingramcontent.com/pod-product-compliance
Lightning Source LLC
Chambersburg PA
CBHW041235060526
44107CB00136BA/738